Sandy Ransford was born in Yorkshire and worked in publishing in London before becoming a full-time writer. She has written many titles for children, including books on animals, ponies and riding, conservation, spies and codes, magic, puzzles, quizzes, games, jokes and activities. She now lives on a smallholding in mid-Wales with her husband, who is an architect, plus two small ponies, two pygmy goats, two pet sheep and a cat.

Strawberrie Donnelly has been a designer and illustrator of children's books for as long as she can remember. She loves drawing fairies and also bears, tigers and ponies; all the pets she's not allowed to have! Strawberrie lives by the sea in Brighton, East Sussex, with Basil the Bearded Collie. They both enjoy long walks, sunshine and chocolate biscuits.

Fairies

Jokes, Puzzles and Things to Make and Do

by Sandy Ransford

Illustrated by
Strawberrie Donnelly

MACMILLAN CHILDREN'S BOOKS

First published 2007 by Macmillan Children's Books
a division of Macmillan Publishers Limited
20 New Wharf Road, London N1 9RR
Basingstoke and Oxford
www.panmacmillan.com

Associated companies throughout the world

ISBN: 978-0-330-43980-0

1 3 5 7 9 8 6 4 2

A CIP catalogue record for this book is available from
the British Library.

Typeset by Nigel Hazle
Printed and bound in Great Britain by Mackays of Chatham plc, Kent

Contents

Fairy Jokes

Can you make sense of these silly riddles?

Why do fairies find it hard to
talk in front of a goat?
It always butts in!

Why is a fairy's nose in the
middle of her face?
Because it's the (s)centre!

Where was the goblin when
the lights went out?
In the dark!

What is the best thing to put
in fairy cakes?
 Your teeth!

1

Hidden Elves

How many elves are there hidden in this picture?

There are __17__ elves.

Fairy Blessings

These two pictures show a fairy waving her wand to cast a good spell over a sleeping

A

child. How many differences can you spot between them? Look carefully – you should be able to find six.

B

In Fairyland

See if you can find all the fairy words listed below in the grid on the opposite page. The words may read across, up or down, either forwards or backwards, but not diagonally, and they are all in straight lines.

DWARF

ELF

FAIRY QUEEN
(two lines)

FLYING

GNOME

GOBLIN

HOBGOBLIN

IMP

LEPRECHAUN

MAGIC

PIXIE

SPELL

SPRITE

WAND

WINGS

G	O	B	L	I	N	L	A	H
N	F	A	I	R	Y	E	B	O
O	I	M	P	C	D	P	G	B
M	A	G	I	C	L	R	N	G
E	N	M	X	T	P	E	I	O
S	P	R	I	T	E	C	Y	B
N	S	P	E	L	L	H	L	L
P	D	W	A	R	F	A	F	I
T	N	L	N	E	E	U	Q	N
S	G	N	I	W	A	N	D	M

Yo-Yo Ho!

These pixies are having fun playing with yo-yos, but the toys' strings have got all tangled up. Can you work out which toy belongs to which pixie?

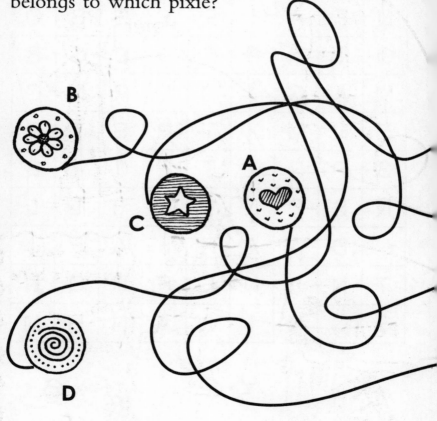

Polly

Peter

Penny

Paul

write your
answers here

Polly ~~D~~

Peter ~~C~~

Penny ~~A~~

Paul ~~B~~

Spot the Real Fairy

It can be difficult to know if a fairy is real or not. Look at the ones on these pages. If a real fairy carries a wand, has two

A

B

C

D

pairs of wings like a butterfly, wears a dress covered in sparkles and a crown with three points, which of the creatures shown is the real fairy?

The real fairy is _E_.

Fairies Fly

Here's a game you can enjoy playing with your friends. Any number can play, and it's great for a party. Ask an adult to be the leader for the first round and call out the instructions until you know how to do it.

This is how you play.

1. All the players sit on the floor and put both hands on the ground. You must keep your hands on the ground unless the leader mentions a creature that flies, such as a fairy. When they do, the players must raise both hands up in the air.

Fairies fly!   Sparrows fly

Sparrows fly

Fairies fly!

2. So, if the leader says, 'Fairies fly,' you must all put your hands up in the air. If they say, 'Sparrows fly,' or 'Blackbirds fly,' you must put your hands up in the air. But if they say, 'Cabbages fly,' you must keep your hands on the ground, and if you don't, then you're out of the game.

3. The last player left in wins, and becomes the leader for the next round.

Sparrows fly

Blackbirds fly

Blackbirds fly

Fairies fly!

Cabbages fly

Fairies fly!

Cabbages fly

Cinderella

Once there was a rich gentleman who had a beautiful, kind daughter. Her mother had died when she was very young, and her father had brought her up on his own. But he thought she needed a mother, so he married a widow, who had two daughters of her own. These girls were ugly and cruel. They bullied the man's daughter and made her do all the housework. The poor girl had to dress in rags and sleep among the cinders on the hearth, and because of this they called her Cinderella.

One day an invitation arrived from

the royal palace – the king was holding a grand ball so his son could choose a bride. The ugly sisters made a great fuss about getting ready, but Cinderella wasn't allowed to go. She had to stay behind and do her work.

The two ugly sisters laughed at Cinderella as they left. She sat sobbing by the fire - but then she heard a soft and gentle voice. Cinderella looked up. She couldn't believe her eyes! A real fairy with a wand was standing in front of her! The fairy told Cinderella she was her fairy godmother, and that Cinderella must fetch a pumpkin, a lizard and six white mice. Then the fairy waved her magic wand and – whoosh! – the pumpkin turned into a glittering golden coach, the lizard into a finely dressed coachman,

15

and the mice into six beautiful white horses. Then she waved her wand again. Cinderella's rags vanished, and she was wearing a sparkling blue and gold ballgown, with delicate glass slippers on her feet.

'There!' beamed the fairy godmother. 'Now go and make your dreams come true. But remember, the magic will fade on the last stroke of midnight – you'll be back in your old clothes, and your coach will turn into a pumpkin again. So you must be sure to leave before then.'

As Cinderella stepped daintily into the ballroom, every head turned to look at her. The king's son was enchanted by her and danced with her all evening. No one recognized her.

The time sped by until the clock began to chime twelve. Suddenly Cinderella remembered her fairy godmother's words, and ran out of the palace, before her dress turned to rags. As she did so, she lost one of her slippers on the palace steps.

The prince tried to catch up with her, but she had gone. He picked up the slipper and vowed to take it to every house in the kingdom until he found the girl whose foot it fitted. How Cinderella's sisters tried to squeeze and squash their feet into the slipper when it was their turn, but the shoe wouldn't fit.

Then Cinderella entered the room. Her face was covered in soot, and her clothes were tattered, but as soon as her foot slid into the slipper the prince knew he had found his bride. And so they got married and lived happily ever after.

Flutter By

How many butterflies in the picture are flying to the right, and how many are flying to the left?

□ Right   ☑ Left

19

Don't Tread on the Daisies!

Can you find a path across this lawn
without treading on any of the daisies?

Find the Fairy

Each line of the poem gives you a letter, and when you write them all down in order they spell out the name of a very well-known fairy.

My first is in teatime, but
never in lunch,

**My second's in icing,
but never in munch.**

My third is in acorn and
also in bean,

**My fourth is in king,
but never in queen.**

My fifth's found in ever,
over and eel,

My sixth begins rover, river and reel.

My seventh sounds like an insect that stings,

My eighth is in necklace, but never in rings.

My ninth and my tenth finish sandal and shawl,

My whole is the best-known fairy of all!

I am: T I N K E R B E L L.

Solve a Crossword

See if you can solve all the clues and fill in the answers in the grid opposite. The numbers in brackets show the number of letters in each word.

Across

1. Crunchy fruit we eat raw and also make into pies (5)

4. Spring flower that grows in woodland – it begins with a colour (8)

8. She gives you a coin when you leave a lost tooth under your pillow (5, 5)

10. Character in *The Wind in the Willows* who loved the river (5)

11. Bird that swims on ponds (4)

13. Across and **2. Down** Fairy from *The Nutcracker* ballet (5, 4)

15. We write it and post it (6)

Down

2. See **13. Across**

3. Adam's wife – and the night before Christmas (3)

4. Yellow flower that grows in fields – it begins with something to eat (9)

5. A wash in a tub full of water (4)

6. A small reptile that lives in warm countries – and the name of part of Cornwall (6)

7. Home for a canary or a budgerigar (8)

9. The opposite of 'in' (3)

12. Frozen water (3)

14. Painting and drawing (3)

Baby Animals

Young animals are usually called by special names. Can you match the animals shown in the pictures with the names of their young?

A

B

C

D

E

F

G

H

Write your answers here

Puppy ___G___

Kitten ___H___

Foal ___E___

Calf ___F___

Lamb ___D___

Cub ___A___

Kid ___G___ C

Fawn ___B___

27

Red Riding Hood

Two rectangles of this picture of Red Riding Hood going to visit her granny are exactly the same. Can you spot which ones they are?

Jokes to Make You Laugh

Why did the goblin swim
with his socks on?
**Because the water was
cold.**

Why did the fairy cut a
hole in her umbrella?
**So she could see when it
had stopped raining.**

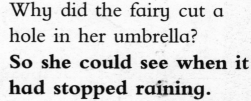

What's the best place for a
fairy to hide a chocolate?
In her mouth!

What's yellow and white
and flies round the world?
**Santa Claus's egg
sandwich.**

29

Santa's Elves

Here is a picture of Santa's elves packing
presents into his sleigh. Time yourself
with a watch while you study the picture
for a whole minute. Then turn the book
upside down and see if you can answer the
questions on this page.

1. How many elves are in the picture?
2. What is the elf with the pointed hat
   putting into the sack?
3. How many parcels are wrapped with
   ribbon?
4. What does Santa have in his hand?
5. How many reindeer are harnessed to
   the sleigh?
6. What is the elf with the spotted jacket
   wearing on his head?

Which Fairy?

Which fairy shown in the pictures below and opposite is the one shown in outline at the top of this page? Study them carefully before you decide.

A

B

C

Make Your Own Wand

Here's how to make a real fairy wand.

You will need:
30 cm narrow cane or dowelling
silver paint (optional)
kitchen foil
cardboard
pencil
scissors
sticky tape
gold curling ribbon (sold for
wrapping presents)
glue
gold stick-on stars

1. Paint the cane or dowelling silver, or cover it with kitchen foil.

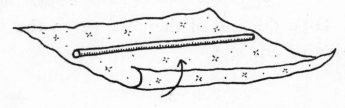

2. Trace the star shown here, then transfer the shape twice to the cardboard. Ask an adult to cut the two cardboard stars out for you.

3. Cover each cardboard star with foil.

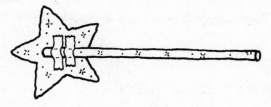

4. Tape the end of the cane on to the inside of one star.

5. Then glue or tape three pieces of ribbon to the inside of the other star. You can curl them round a pencil first if you like.

6. Glue the insides of both stars together, with the handle and ribbon between them. Put a piece of paper over the star, then put a heavy book on top to press all the pieces together until the glue has set.

7. Stick little peel-off gold stars on both sides of the big silver star.

Flying Fairies

Here's a game to play at a party with your friends. You need an odd number of players so one can be the leader who calls out instructions, or an adult can do this.

1. Each player chooses a partner.

2. The leader calls out instructions, such as: 'Sit on the floor,' 'Hold right hands,' 'Stand back to back,' 'Tap your right foot on the ground,' and the players must obey them.

3. This continues until the leader suddenly calls out, 'Flying fairies!' Then the players must run round the room trying to find a new partner. The leader also tries to find a partner.

4. Whoever is left without a partner becomes the leader for the next round, and the game continues.

Princess in the Tower

How many differences can you spot between these two pictures of a princess in a tower?

A

Look carefully – you should be able to find six.

B

Very Silly Books

Freda the fairy has some very funny books on her shelves! Let's look at them.

Growing Vegetables — ROSA CARROTS

KEEPING TIDY — ANITA HOUSE

Polar Explorations — Ann Tarctic

Collecting Litter — PHIL D. BASKET

EMBARRASSING MOMENTS — LUCY LASTIC

Flying Lessons — HUGO FIRST

Millionaire Fairy — IVOR FORTUNE

Make a Collection

Do you like collecting things? See if you can find all the things in the list during the next week. You could have a competition with a friend to see who can collect them all first.

1. A picture of a toadstool (it could be in a book).

2. If it's summer, ten daisies. If it's winter, ten dried leaves.

3. A bird's feather.

4. A gold sweet wrapper.

5. A new joke (it could be in this book!).

6. A green hat.

Snow White

A long time ago there was a princess with skin as white as snow, lips as red as blood and hair as black as ebony. She was called Snow White.

Her stepmother was the queen, and she was beautiful but cruel and vain. She would stand in front of her magic mirror, saying, 'Mirror, mirror, on the wall, who is the fairest of them all?' And the mirror would always answer, 'In this land there is none fairer than you, o Queen.' This made the queen happy.

But one day the mirror replied: 'You are beautiful, o Queen, 'tis true, but Snow White is now more fair than you.' The queen was very angry, and envious of Snow White. So she ordered a servant to take Snow White into the forest and kill her.

But the servant was fond of Snow White and could not harm her. So when they got into the forest he let her go free.

She ran until she came to a little cottage. Everything inside was very small.

On the table were seven little plates and seven little mugs. Against the wall stood seven little beds. Snow White was puzzled, but she was so tired that she lay down and went to sleep.

When night fell, the owners of the cottage returned home. They were seven dwarfs, and they were so enchanted by Snow White that they invited her to stay with them.

Back at the castle, when the queen next consulted her magic mirror, it said, 'O Queen, you are the fairest of all I see, but in the woods, where the seven dwarfs dwell, Snow White is alive and well, and none is fairer than she.' The queen exploded with rage. Snow White had to die!

She poisoned an apple. Then she dressed as an old beggar woman and went to the forest to find Snow White.

Snow White knew the queen wanted her dead and that she should not open the door to a stranger, but the beggar woman's apple looked delicious, so Snow White opened the door and took it. But as soon as she bit into it, she fell down dead.

The dwarfs made Snow White a glass coffin so they could watch over her. One day a prince came riding by. He saw Snow White and fell in love with her. He lifted her up out of the coffin, and as he did so, the piece of poisoned apple fell from her mouth. Restored to life, Snow White sat up, saw the prince and fell in love with him. So she waved goodbye to her beloved dwarfs and went with the prince to his palace to become his bride.

Tea Party

Look carefully at these four pictures of a
fairy tea party. One picture contains

A

B

two things that aren't in the other three. Can you spot what they are, and which picture they are in? *A + D*

C

D

Did You Know?

Bet you didn't know all these fairy facts.

Way back in 1917 two girls took photographs of fairies, which Sir Arthur Conan Doyle, the author of the Sherlock Holmes stories, published in a magazine. He was sure they were genuine. But in 1983 the girls, by this time old ladies, explained that they had taken photographs of cut-out fairies they had carefully positioned in the garden.

Irish fairies are called leprechauns. People think they were shoemakers. They also believe the leprechauns carried purses containing just one shilling (now 12.5 pence).

Pixies come from Devon and Cornwall, where they are sometimes called piskies.

Brownies are little fairies that live in people's homes and help with the housework at night. Are there any in your house?

Dwarfs live in rocky caves, where they guard minerals like gold and precious stones such as diamonds.

Elves are similar to dwarfs. They are often mischievous, and they can be good or bad.

Gnomes are also similar to dwarfs. They are often ugly and strangely shaped.

Find the Girls

You can trace out all the girls' names listed below in the grid opposite. They may read across, up, down or diagonally, either forwards or backwards, but they are all in straight lines. Use a pencil and a ruler to help you find them.

ABIGAIL	IRIS
ALICE	JENNY
ANGELA	JILL
BRIDGET	KAY
CATHY	KYLIE
CLAIRE	LUCY
ELERI	SALLY
ELIZABETH	SOPHIE
EMILY	TESSA
EMMA	TILLY
GEMMA	ZARA
HELEN	

E	C	C	A	T	H	Y	N	K
M	L	J	J	E	N	N	Y	A
M	A	I	K	S	A	L	L	Y
A	I	L	Z	S	B	D	U	J
B	R	L	A	A	L	I	C	E
R	E	Y	R	B	B	H	Y	S
I	D	L	A	I	D	E	N	O
D	N	I	G	G	S	L	T	P
G	E	M	M	A	I	E	I	H
E	L	E	R	I	R	N	L	I
T	T	K	Y	L	I	E	L	E
A	N	G	E	L	A	D	Y	N

Make Your Own Fairy Crown

Here's how to make a gold or silver crown so you can be a real fairy princess.

You will need:
measuring tape
thin gold or silver card
scissors
coloured foil stickers for decoration
sticky tape

You will need an adult to help you with this.

1. Ask an adult to measure round your head.

2. Measure out the same length on the cardboard and add 3 cm. Ask an adult to cut out a band of cardboard this length and about 5 cm wide.

3. Ask an adult to help you try on the crown, overlap the ends at the back and mark by how much the ends overlap. Then ask them to cut halfway up one end, and halfway down the other, so the ends can slot together, as shown in the diagram.

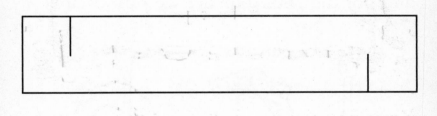

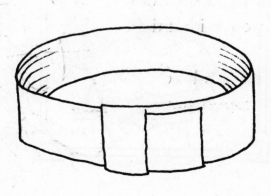

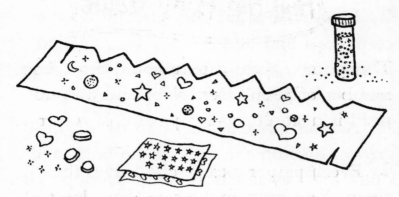

4. Ask an adult to cut points in the crown with scissors. Then decorate your crown with coloured stick-on stars or other shapes and slot the ends together to form a circle.

Find-the-Fairy Game

This game is fun to play at a party. Any number of people can play, and all you need is a small cut-out picture of a fairy.

1. Every player except one leaves the room. You must make sure they don't peek!

2. The player left in the room puts the fairy picture somewhere in the room. It must not be hidden, but it shouldn't be too easy to see.

3. The other players come in and start looking for the fairy. If anyone spots it, they say nothing, but just sit down.

4. The last player left standing has to pay a forfeit, for example, drawing a fairy of their own, or singing a song.

Knock, Knock!

Have a good laugh at these fairy knock, knock jokes.

Knock, knock.
Who's there?
Fairy.
Fairy who?
Fairy Nuff.

Knock, knock.
Who's there?
Ena.
Ena who?
Ena minute the fairies will arrive.

Knock, knock.
Who's there?
Sam.
Sam who?
Sam fairy who knocked
yesterday.

Knock, knock.
Who's there?
Ivor.
Ivor who?
Ivor new pair of wings. Do
you like them?

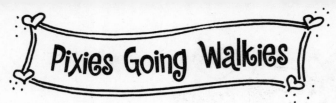

Pixies Going Walkies

These pixies are taking their dogs for a walk, but the dogs' leads have got tangled up. Can you work out which dog belongs to which pixie?

Riley

Rover

Roger

Rex

Poppy

Patrick

Posie

Philip

write your
answers here

Poppy _pRuey_

Patrick _paver_

Posie _Rof_

Philip _Royer_

59

Patchwork Quilt

The mummy fairy is sewing a quilt for her baby's bed. She has collected feathers, leaves and petals from many different birds and plants. How many different patterns can you spot in the quilt? Count them and colour each pattern in a different colour.

There are _____ patterns.

Twin Unicorns

Which two of the unicorns shown here are exactly the same?

A

B

C

D

Journey I-Spy

You may not see a unicorn, but next time you go on a journey by car, bus or train, see how many of the following things you can spot when you are looking out of the window.

1. A tree with blossom (in spring), or one with bright yellow leaves (in autumn).

2. A dog herding sheep.

3. A red and yellow lorry.

4. A double-decker bus.

5. Four or more ponies in a field.

6. A level crossing (where a road crosses a railway track).

7. A helicopter.

8. A bridge over a river.

Classroom Jokes

Even fairies have to go to school! Here are some favourite jokes from fairy classrooms.

When does 7 + 7 equal 13?
When you can't add up!

TEACHER: How do you spell 'mouse'?
SAMMY: Er, M, O, U, S . . .
TEACHER: Yes, but what's at the end of it?
SAMMY: Er, a tail?

TEACHER: Susie! Didn't you hear me call you?
SUSIE: Yes, miss, but you told us we mustn't answer back.

TEACHER: Why don't you write more clearly?
FREDDIE: Because then you'd realize I can't spell!

Good Fairy, Bad Fairy

Who will get to the animals first — the good fairy or the bad fairy? Stay away from the toadstools!

Scary Ring

Beauty and the Beast

Once there was a rich merchant who had a very pretty daughter called Beauty.

One day, when returning home, the merchant lost his way in a storm. Luckily he came to a brightly lit castle that seemed to be deserted. Weak and tired, he tucked into a meal that lay on the table and fell asleep.

The next day, as he was leaving the castle, the merchant went to pick a rose for Beauty from the garden. Suddenly a terrible voice roared at him, 'How dare you?!' Facing him was a fierce and terrifying Beast. 'I have given you shelter and in return you steal my roses!'

'But it was for my daughter,' pleaded the merchant.

'Bring her to me,' the Beast roared. 'Otherwise I will find and eat you both!'

So when the merchant returned home, he took his daughter back to the Beast's castle. At the sight of the Beast, Beauty felt faint with terror, but he made her welcome, and merely asked her to sit with him and talk to him each evening.

As the days passed, Beauty came to enjoy her evenings with the Beast. The only problem was that every evening the Beast asked her to marry him. And every evening Beauty refused: she had grown fond of the Beast, but how could she marry him?

Though she was happy, Beauty missed her father. The Beast had a magic mirror,

and one day, when Beauty looked in it, she saw a picture of her father looking gravely ill. Because the Beast loved Beauty so much, he said she could go home. 'But,' he said softly, 'you must return within seven days or I shall die of grief.'

So Beauty went home, and her father was soon much better. But after nine days had passed, Beauty had a dream. She saw the Beast lying on the ground as if he was truly dying of grief. So she rushed back to his castle, ran to his side and covered his face with kisses. 'What do looks matter

compared with a kind and gentle heart?'
she cried. 'Live, dear Beast, and I will
marry you!'

With these words, the Beast opened his
eyes and, as he did so, he turned into a
handsome prince. Beauty's love had broken
a spell cast by a wicked fairy. So she
married her Beast and they had a long and
happy life together.

Tiara Test

These pictures of a fairy tiara may all look the same, but one of them is different from all the others. Which one is it?

Tiara _____

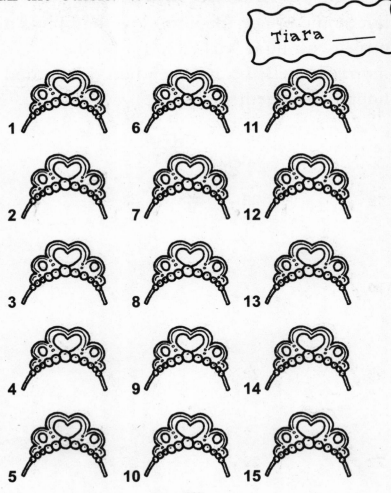

1

2

3

4

5

6

7

8

9

10

11

12

13

14

15

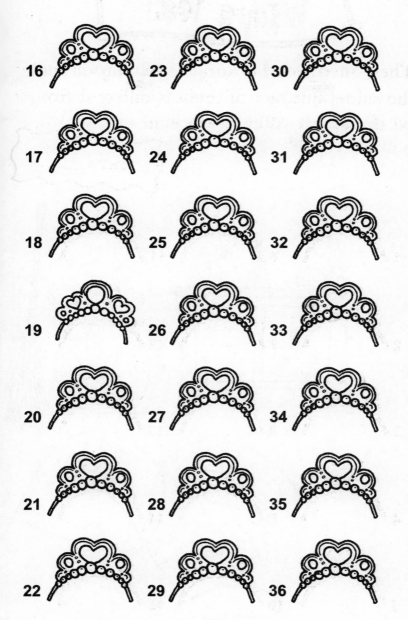

Which Is Which?

These three witches are busy knitting, but the naughty kitten has muddled up their wool! Which witch is knitting with which ball of wool?

Write your answers here

A ___23___ C ___2___
B ___1___

How Many Words?

How many words can you make from the letters that make up the word FAIRYLAND? You could start with FAIRY and LAND, and then there are words such as:

RAY, NAIL, and **ANY**.

See how many you can find. More than ten is good, more than 20 is excellent.

Fairy, Land, Ray, nail, any, And AIR FAIR FAN YARN AIRY FLAN FAIL AIL RAID RAIN RAIL FAY DAIRY DIARY DAAL

Fairy Food Chuckles

Have a laugh at these fairy food jokes.

What do fairies put in cakes?
Elf-raising flour.

FIRST FAIRY: I feel like a cup of tea.
SECOND FAIRY: You look like one too – you're all wet and sloppy.

How do pixies eat?
By gobblin'.

What did the pixie's cat like for breakfast?
Mice Krispies.

You can find all the foods listed below in the grid opposite. The words may read across, up or down, either forwards or backwards, but not diagonally, and they are all in straight lines. Use a pencil and a ruler to help you find them.

APPLES
BACON
CAKE
CHEESE
CHIPS
CHOCOLATE
CURRY
CUSTARD
EGGS
FISH

GRAPES
HOT DOGS
ICE CREAM
JELLY
MILK
ORANGES
PIZZA
SAUSAGES
SOUP

C	H	O	C	O	L	A	T	E
U	O	I	D	F	I	S	H	G
S	T	C	H	E	E	S	E	G
T	D	E	B	A	C	O	N	S
A	O	C	C	P	J	N	B	O
R	G	R	A	P	E	S	C	R
D	S	E	K	L	L	P	U	A
K	O	A	E	E	L	I	R	N
L	U	M	J	S	Y	H	R	G
I	P	I	Z	Z	A	C	Y	E
M	S	A	U	S	A	G	E	S

Cinderella's Slipper

Can you spot the odd one out?

slipper _____

1

2

3

4

5

6

80

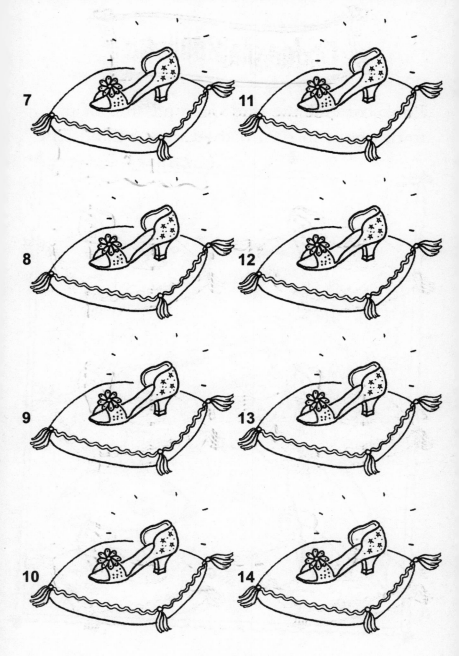

Magic Spell 1

Look carefully at these two pictures of a fairy about to turn a toad into a handsome

A

prince. How many differences are there between the pictures? Look carefully – you should be able to find six.

B

More Silly Jokes

Where are fairy queens
crowned?
On their heads!

 What time is it when a fairy's
clock strikes 13?
 Time she got a new clock!

What do fairies call little white
cats?
Kittens!

 What is a fairy after it's two
years old?
Three years old!

Terrible Tongue Twisters

Try saying each of these slowly six times, and see if you can do it without making a mistake!

Three free-flying fairies flew flittering from three trees.

Swan, swim over the sea.
Swim, swan, swim!
Swan, swim back over the sea,
Well swum, swan!

Greedy goblins gobbled grapes grumpily.

Philly the silly fairy wore pink silk socks with spots.

Which of these fairy toadstools is the odd one out?

Toadstool _16_

Sleeping Beauty

Once upon a time, there was a king and a queen who longed to have a baby. So when they did have a daughter they were so overjoyed that they held a magnificent feast.

As was the custom in those days, twelve good fairies came to present their gifts to the baby. They granted her virtue, beauty, riches and many other good things.

But as the twelfth fairy was about to present her gift, in came an evil thirteenth fairy, who was furious at not having been invited. 'Here is my gift,' she said spitefully.

'When this little princess is fifteen, she will prick her finger with a spindle and fall down dead!'

Everyone was very shocked. But the twelfth fairy stepped forward. 'I cannot undo the evil magic completely,' she said, 'but your daughter will not die. Instead she will fall into a deep sleep that will last a hundred years.'

As the years passed, the princess grew into a beautiful, kind young girl. On her fifteenth birthday she decided to explore the castle where she lived. She climbed a staircase up a tower and at the top she found a tiny room. Inside, an old lady was sitting at a spinning wheel.

'Come and try your hand at spinning,' said the lady, but as soon as the princess touched the spindle, she pricked her finger and fell into a deep sleep. Then, one by one, everyone in the castle fell asleep. The building and the grounds were neglected. A huge thorn hedge grew round the boundary. Gradually the strange story of the Sleeping Beauty spread throughout the land. Many princes tried to cut down the hedge and enter the castle to see if the rumours were true, but the thorns were too thick and strong for them.

But exactly one hundred years later, another prince arrived. He slashed at the hedge with his sword, and, as he did so, every thorn turned into a rose and a way through the hedge opened up for him.

He walked through the castle full of sleeping people, found the entrance to the highest tower and climbed the stairs.

In the little room at the top, he saw Sleeping

Beauty and he bent down to kiss her. As soon as he did so, her eyes opened and love filled both their hearts.

The evil fairy's curse had been lifted, and the whole castle woke up and started going about their daily lives as if nothing had ever happened.

Sleeping Beauty and the prince had a wonderful wedding celebration, and they lived happily every after.

Funny Noises

Here are some pictures and words describing noises, but the words have been put with the wrong pictures. Can you match up the words with the correct pictures?

C

Rrringgg!

D

Splash!

Write your   A ___C___   C ___B___
answers here B ___D___   D ___B___

93

Find the Boys

All the boys' names listed below can be traced out in the grid opposite. The words may read across, up, down or diagonally, either forwards or backwards, but they are all in straight lines. Use a pencil and a ruler to help you find them.

ANDREW
COLIN
DAMIAN
DAVID
EDWARD
HARRY
JACK
JASON
LIONEL
MARK

MATTHEW
MICHAEL
NEIL
NICHOLAS
OLIVER
PETER
ROBERT
ROBIN
ROSS
WILLIAM

J	K	W	E	H	T	T	A	M
A	D	I	V	A	D	L	A	I
C	O	L	I	N	K	R	N	C
K	J	L	N	Y	K	O	I	H
A	B	I	O	R	D	B	C	A
N	J	A	L	R	N	E	H	E
D	A	M	I	A	N	R	O	L
R	S	P	V	H	T	T	L	I
E	O	P	E	T	E	R	A	O
W	N	G	R	O	S	S	S	N
J	K	L	D	R	A	W	D	E
S	R	O	B	I	N	E	I	L

Pussy Cat, Pussy Cat

Enjoy these silly cat jokes!

Which pantomime is about a cat in a chemist's shop?
Puss in Boots.

What happened to the cat that ate a ball of wool?
She had mittens.

What do you get if you cross a cat with a sea creature?
An octo-puss.

What do cats like to read?
Mewspapers.

Puss in Boots

Look at this picture of *Puss in Boots*. Three of the squares are exactly the same. Can you spot which ones they are?

Riddle Me Ree

Solve the verse riddle to find two well-known fairy tale and pantomime characters.

My first is in tub, but
never in toy,

**My second's in girl, but
never in boy.**

My third begins lolly, lazy
and less,

**My fourth asks a
question and starts the
word 'yes'.**

My fifth is in hisses, lasses
and bees,

**My sixth sounds like an
organ that sees.**

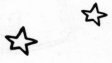

My seventh's the same as
my fifth, so we think,

**My eighth is a meal,
and also a drink.**

My ninth begins eagle,
earwig and eel,

**My tenth begins rabbit,
robin and reel.**

My last is the same as my
fifth, once again,

**My whole is two girls
who are both quite a
pain!**

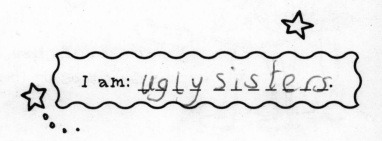

I am: _ugly sisters._

Way Out

Can you help Hansel and Gretel find their way out of the wood?

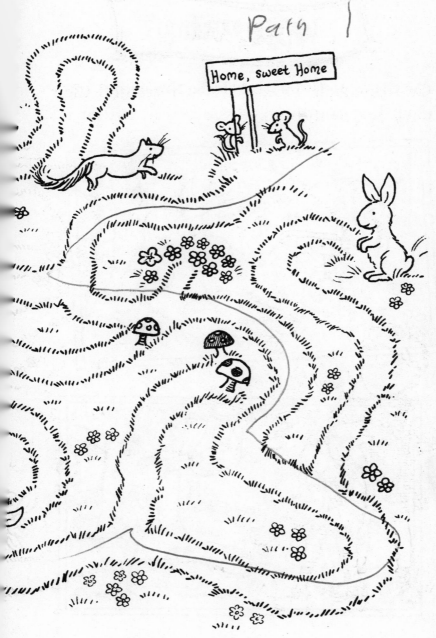

Home, sweet Home

101

What's Missing?

All these pictures may look the same, but each has one thing missing from it that is

1

2

in all the others — a different thing in each picture. Can you spot what's missing in each picture?

3

4

Word Snake

You can trace out all the fairy-tale characters listed below in the grid opposite. The arrow marks the start, and the words go in one continuous line, snaking up and down, backwards and forwards, but never diagonally. Use a pencil to trace the snake.

CINDERELLA
FAIRY GODMOTHER
FROG PRINCE
GRETEL
HANSEL
RUMPELSTILTSKIN
SNOW QUEEN
TINKERBELL

C	I	N	D	Y	G	O	D
L	E	R	E	R	T	O	M
L	A	F	A	I	H	E	R
L	L	I	T	N	E	E	F
B	E	N	O	W	Q	U	R
R	E	K	N	R	P	G	O
K	I	N	S	I	N	C	E
S	T	L	I	T	E	R	G
E	L	S	T	E	L	H	A
P	M	U	R	L	E	S	N

Frog Prince

Not every frog can be turned into a prince.
Only those with dark stones in the centres
of their crowns and two toes on their front
legs can become princes. Among all the
frogs on these pages, how many can be
turned into princes?

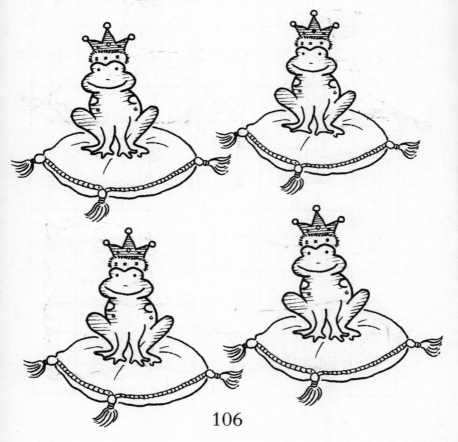

write
your
answer
here

___

Fairy Wheel Sandwiches

These little sandwiches are just like the ones fairies eat. They are perfect for a party.

You will need:
sliced bread
knife
a rolling pin
butter or other spread
your favourite filling

1. Ask an adult to trim the crusts off the bread.

2. Put each slice on the bread board and flatten it out with the rolling pin.

3. Spread the butter (or spread) on the bread. Add your favourite filling. This could be cheese, ham, tomato, egg, Marmite – whatever you like. Don't put too much filling on the bread or it will fall off when you roll it up.

4. Roll up each slice of bread as tightly as you can.

109

5. Put the rolls to chill in the refrigerator for about 45 minutes.

6. Get out the rolls and ask an adult to slice them thinly into rounds to make little wheel shapes.

More Fairy Chuckles

Why did the silly fairy put honey on her pillow?
So she would have sweet dreams.

What do you call an elf that lives with his granny and grandpa?
An old folks' gnome.

Why did the fairy bees hum?
Because they couldn't remember the words.

FAIRY SISTER: How did Mum know you hadn't had a wash?
FAIRY BROTHER: I forgot to wet the soap.

Drawing Game

This game is a lot of fun at a party or when you have friends round.

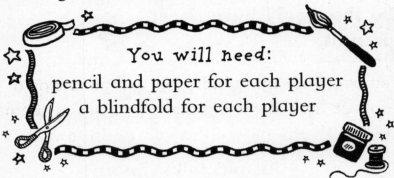

You will need:
pencil and paper for each player
a blindfold for each player

1. Each player sits at a table with a sheet of paper and a pencil.

2. Someone puts a blindfold round each player's eyes.

3. The players are told to draw a picture of a fairy castle.

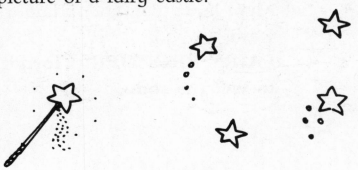

4. When they've done that, they are asked to draw some clouds in the sky behind the castle.

5. Then they're asked to draw a fairy in front of the castle.

6. When everyone has finished, they remove their blindfolds and everyone has a look at their drawings and then passes them round. Everyone will have a good laugh!

Magic Spell 2

Remember the pictures of a fairy starting to turn a toad into a prince on pages 82–3?

A

Well, here she's succeeded. How many differences can you spot between these two pictures? Look carefully, you should be able to find six.

B

Find the Wild Flowers

Some people think fairies live in wild flowers. The names of all the flowers listed below can be traced out in the grid opposite. The words may read across, up or down, either forwards or backwards, but not diagonally, and they are all in straight lines.

BLUEBELL
BUTTERCUP
COWSLIP
DAFFODIL
DAISY
FOXGLOVE
HAREBELL

HONEYSUCKLE
IRIS
MOONPENNY
POPPY
PRIMROSE
ROSE
SNOWDROP

H	A	R	E	B	E	L	L	M
O	R	C	S	U	S	L	P	O
N	O	O	O	T	N	E	O	O
E	S	W	R	T	O	B	P	N
Y	E	S	M	E	W	E	P	P
S	N	L	I	R	D	U	Y	E
U	S	I	R	C	R	L	S	N
C	I	P	P	U	O	B	I	N
K	R	R	N	P	P	D	A	Y
L	I	D	O	F	F	A	D	D
E	V	O	L	G	X	O	F	N

Flower Fairies

Many of the flowers in this picture have a fairy hidden in them. Can you spot how many fairies there are?

There are _____ fairies.

The Princess and the Pea

Once upon a time there was a young prince who wanted a wife, but he did not want just any girl. Oh no. His bride had to be a real princess. So he travelled round the world to try to find one. He met many so-called princesses – some who were genuine but who were not pretty, or sweet, or clever enough, and others who seemed right but who were not princesses at all, but were just pretending to be because they wanted to marry a prince.

Despairing of finding a suitable bride, the prince returned home alone.

Then one evening a terrible storm raged. There was thunder and lightning, and the rain fell in torrents.

Suddenly there was a knock at the palace door and the king went to open it. Outside stood a pretty girl asking for shelter from the storm. Her hair and clothes were soaking wet and her shoes were muddy, but she said she was a princess so the king let her in.

'I'll soon find out if she is a real princess,' said the wise old queen. She went to the guest room and placed a tiny pea on the bed. Then she ordered twenty mattresses to be placed on top of the bed, and then twenty eiderdowns on top of the mattresses.

They gave the girl dry clothes and supper, and then showed her to the guest room.

The next morning the queen asked, 'And how did you sleep, my dear?'

'Oh, very badly,' the girl replied. 'I was awake most of the night because there was a lump in my bed.'

At that, the king and queen knew that the girl was a real princess – for only a real princess was so sensitive that she could feel a pea through twenty mattresses and twenty eiderdowns. So she and the prince were married. And as for the pea, it was put into a museum where you can still see it to this day.

What's the Time, Mr Wolf?

Here's a game to remind you of Little Red Riding Hood. Any number of people can play.

1. One player is the wolf, and he or she stands facing the wall. The other players go to the opposite side of the room.

2. When the game starts, the players move forwards slowly, chanting, 'What's the time, Mr Wolf?' And the wolf, without turning round, says, 'One o'clock,' or, 'Three o'clock,' or whatever he or she wishes.

3. Then the players creep forwards again, chanting, 'What's the time, Mr Wolf?'

4. The game goes on like this, until the wolf says, 'Dinner time!', turning round and chasing the rest of the players back across the room. If the wolf manages to catch a player, they become the wolf for the next round.

How Many Jewels?

Do you know the story of Aladdin? His genie provided him with many jewels to take to the father of the princess he wished to marry. If the black jewels are rubies, the white ones diamonds and the striped ones emeralds, how many of each type of jewel are there in the picture?

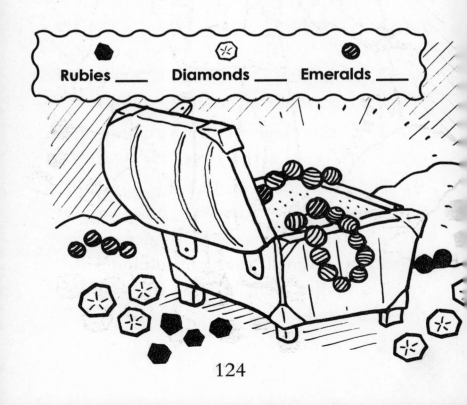

Rubies ____ Diamonds ____ Emeralds ____

Treasure Hunt

Can you find your way through the seaweed to the treasure chest on the seabed?

Fairy-Tale Grid

The names of the fairy-tale characters listed below can be fitted into the grid opposite. Each will only go in one place, and we have given you some letters to help you start. The secret is to count the number of letters in each word and the number of spaces in the grid.

ALADDIN   OGRE
ALI BABA   RIP VAN WINKLE
BEAST   SINDBAD
BEAUTY   SULTAN
GIANT   THREE BEARS

128

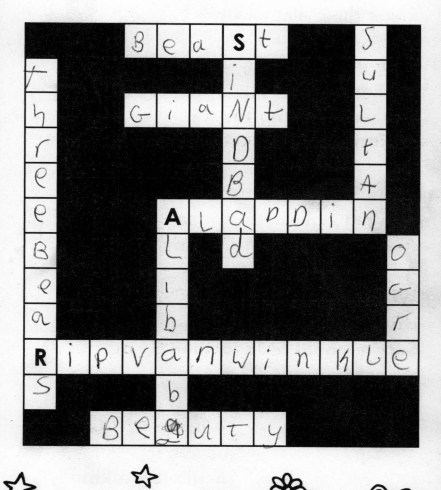

A crossword puzzle grid with the following answers filled in:

- Beast
- Giant
- Sultan
- Aladdin
- threebears
- Ripvanwinkle
- Beauty
- Ogr (Ogre)
- Sindbad (S-i-N-D-B)
- Alibib (A-L-i-b-b)

129

Giggle Time

Enjoy these silly jokes.

Why didn't the silly fairy eat
her hamburger?
**She was waiting for the
mustard to cool.**

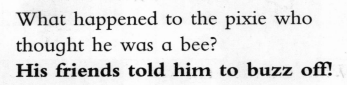

What happened to the pixie who
thought he was a bee?
His friends told him to buzz off!

Why did the fairy wear a
red dress?
**So she could hide in the
strawberry patch.**

What says, 'Muf, if,
of, eef'?
**A giant walking
backwards.**

Why did the fairy wear
sunglasses?
**She didn't want anyone
to recognize her.**

Why couldn't the
witch tell the time?
**She'd lost her
witch-watch.**

What did the very fast
witch ride?
A broom-broom-stick.

How does a fairy start a
jelly race?
She says, 'Get set!'

Flying Fast

How many differences can you spot
between these two pictures of witches flying

A

on broomsticks? Look carefully – you
should be able to find six.

B

Fairy Wands

Three of these fairy wands are different from all the others. Can you spot which three they are?

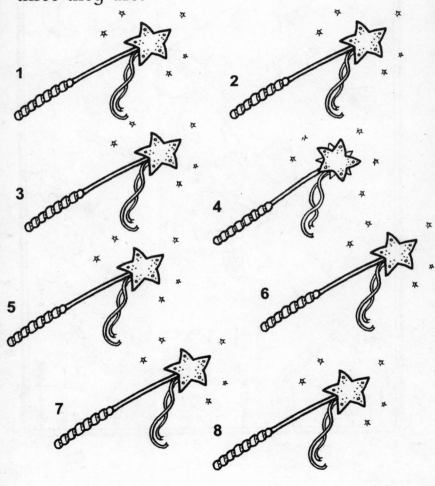

1

2

3

4

5

6

7

8

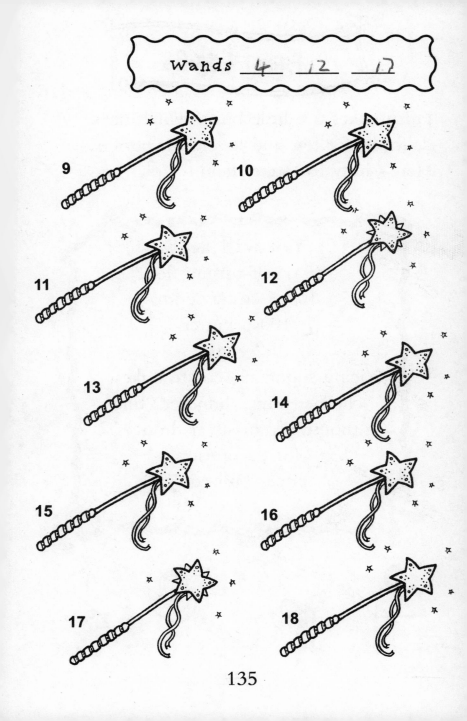

wands 4   12   17

135

Fairy Cakes

Fairy cakes are little buns, which are delicious for tea and lovely for parties. Here's how to make them.

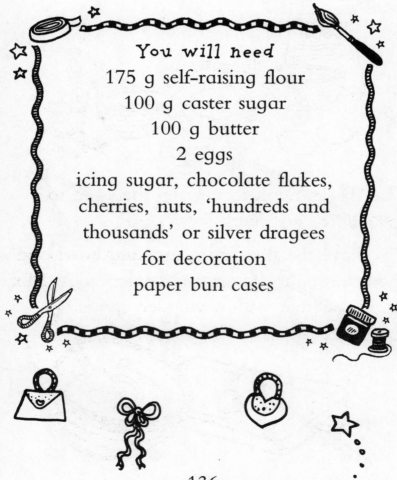

You will need
175 g self-raising flour
100 g caster sugar
100 g butter
2 eggs
icing sugar, chocolate flakes,
cherries, nuts, 'hundreds and
thousands' or silver dragees
for decoration
paper bun cases

1. Measure out all the dry ingredients into separate bowls. Leave the butter in a warm place to soften. Crack the eggs into another bowl (or ask an adult to do this for you), and beat them with a fork.

2. Ask an adult to turn on the oven to 190 °C or gas mark 5.

3. Sieve the flour into a mixing bowl and add the sugar, butter and beaten eggs. Mix it all together with a wooden spoon.

4. Using a teaspoon, drop a heaped spoonful of the mixture into each paper case. Stand the cases on a baking sheet.

5. Ask an adult to put the baking sheet into the oven, and after 12–15 minutes to get the cakes out and stand them on a wire rack until they are cool.

9. Mix the icing sugar with a little water until you have a smooth paste. Spoon a little on to each cake. Decorate with cherries, chopped nuts, little flakes of chocolate or 'hundreds and thousands'.

Fairy Quiz

See if you can answer the questions in this fairy quiz.

1. In which book does Tinkerbell appear?

2. What made Sleeping Beauty sleep for 100 years?

3. How many dwarfs did Snow White have?

4. Which country do leprechauns come from?

5. Who made it possible for Cinderella to go to the ball?

6. What is a fairy ring?

Thumbelina

Once there lived a woman who loved children and very much wanted a child of her own. A witch gave her a magic seed to plant, and it grew into a beautiful flower. Inside sat a tiny girl no bigger than your thumb. The woman named her Thumbelina.

Thumbelina spent her days floating on a pond in a petal boat, and at night she slept in a walnut shell. But one night an ugly toad spotted her and stole her, because he thought she would make a pretty wife for his even uglier son. Luckily some fish

spotted what was happening and took pity
on Thumbelina. They chased off the toad,
and pulled her shell far, far away. Then she
was snatched up by a beetle, who flew off
with her and dropped her in a wide and
lonely forest. But at least she was free. She
passed the summer happily, alone in the
forest, but when autumn began shrivelling
up the leaves and flowers Thumbelina knew
that winter was coming and she would need
shelter. So she walked and walked until
at last she found a door on the edge of a
cornfield. Inside lived a friendly field mouse,
who took her in and fed her.

One day the field mouse said, 'My
neighbour, Mole, is coming to visit. He is

rich and clever. He will be a good husband for you.' Mole built tunnels from the field mouse's den to his own and visited his friend frequently. He fell in love with Thumbelina, but she couldn't love him back. And she hated the thought of having to live underground with him, and never see the sun.

Now it just so happened that one day a swallow fell into one of the tunnels. It was injured, and Thumbelina tended it and nursed it back to health. When spring-time returned, the swallow asked Thumbelina to fly away with him, but she felt she couldn't leave the kind field mouse.

And so her marriage to Mole was fixed. But as the day of the wedding drew near Thumbelina felt sad. How could she marry someone who hated daylight and had no joy in his heart? She went to take her last look at the sun — and there was her friend the swallow! Once again he asked Thumbelina to fly away with him, and this time she agreed. She climbed on his back, he spread his powerful wings and they soared up into the sky.

Eventually they arrived beside a blue lake with flowers growing on its banks. 'Choose a flower,' said the swallow. 'It will become your home.'

Thumbelina chose a large white flower, and the swallow set her down on one of its broad leaves. And as he did so, the flower opened and inside was a tiny man, exactly the same size as her! He wore a gold crown and had delicate wings, for he was the King of the Fairies. When he saw how beautiful Thumbelina was, he asked her to marry him. And this time, Thumbelina happily said, 'Yes!'

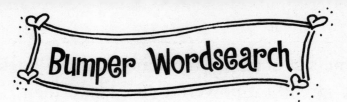

Bumper Wordsearch

The words in this puzzle are all colours, and their names can all be traced out in the grid opposite. The words may run across, up, down or diagonally, either forwards or backwards, but they are all in straight lines. Use a pencil and a ruler to help you find them.

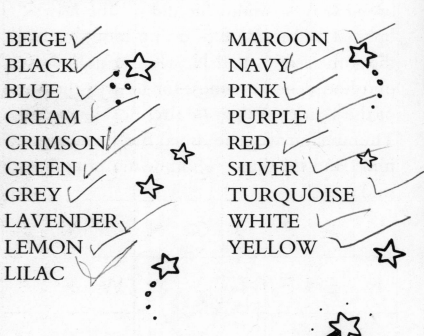

BEIGE

BLACK

BLUE

CREAM

CRIMSON

GREEN

GREY

LAVENDER

LEMON

LILAC

MAROON

NAVY

PINK

PURPLE

RED

SILVER

TURQUOISE

WHITE

YELLOW

C	R	E	A	M	N	B	N	T
R	B	E	I	G	E	G	E	U
I	L	L	N	N	E	R	L	R
M	U	I	A	D	R	E	P	Q
S	E	L	V	C	G	Y	R	U
O	L	A	Y	K	K	E	U	O
N	M	C	R	E	D	L	P	I
O	N	T	R	E	V	L	I	S
M	A	R	O	O	N	O	N	E
E	B	E	T	I	H	W	K	Y
L	A	V	E	N	D	E	R	Z

More Knock, Knocks

Here are more silly jokes to make you laugh.

Knock, knock.
Who's there?
Vera.
Vera who?
Vera bouts do the fairies live?

Knock, knock.
Who's there?
Alec.
Alec who?
Alec your wand.

Knock, knock.
Who's there?
Bernardette.
Bernardette who?
Bernardette all my fairy cakes.

Knock, knock.
Who's there?
Ammonia.
Ammonia who?
Ammonia little fairy and I
can't reach the doorbell.

Knock, knock.
Who's there?
Arthur.
Arthur who?
Arthur any fairies at the
bottom of your garden?

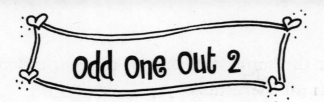

Odd One Out 2

These pictures of a dancing fairy may all

1

2

3

4

look the same, but one of them is different
from all the others.
Which one is it?

Fairy _7_

5

6

7

8

Find the Word

If you solve all the clues correctly and fill in the answers in the grid, the column marked with arrows will show a word meaning a kind of fairy.

1. A naughty little elf or demon. (6 letters)
2. It's worn over your clothes to keep them clean when you are cooking. (5 letters)
3. It fastens a door when you turn a key. (4 letters)
4. A king wears one on his head. (5 letters)
5. A kind of summer shoe. (6 letters)
6. A coach pulled by horses. (8 letters)
7. A slice of it can make toast. (5 letters)

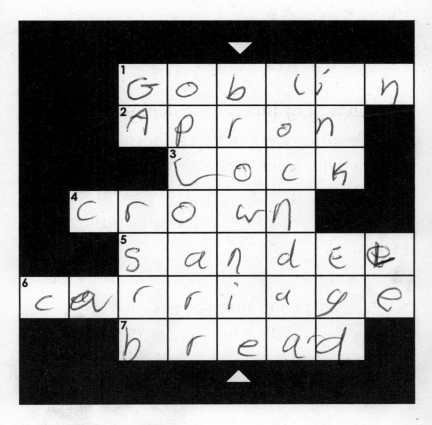

1. Goblin
2. Apron
3. Lock
4. crown
5. sander
6. carriage
7. bread

151

Which Cat?

These pictures of a sitting cat may all

look the same, but one of them is different
from all the others. Which one is it?

6

cat 4

7

8

9

10

Fairy Secrets

Here's a game that's sure to give you a good laugh.

1. All the players sit on the floor in a circle. The first player whispers a fairy secret into the ear of the player on their left. This might be, 'Fairies wear pink shoes,' or, 'Fairies can't fly at night,' or anything else you like.

2. The next player whispers the secret to the player on their left, and the game continues until the secret is whispered to the player just before the one who said it in the first place.

3. This player says the secret out loud, as they heard it, and then the first player says the original secret. They are usually very different!

4. Another player whispers another secret for the next round.

Answers to Puzzles

page 2 – Hidden Elves

There are 19 elves.

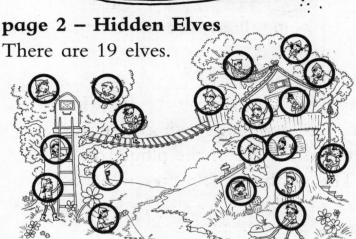

page 4 – Fairy Blessings

page 6 – In Fairyland

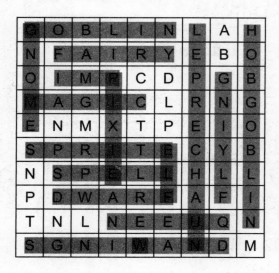

page 8 – Yo-Yo Ho!
Polly – D, Peter – B, Penny – A, Paul – C

page 10 – Spot the Real Fairy
Fairy E is the real fairy.

page 18 – Flutter By
There are 9 butterflies flying to the right
and 12 flying to the left.

page 20 – Don't Tread on the Daisies!

page 22 – Find the Fairy

TINKERBELL

page 24 – Solve a Crossword

page 26 – Baby Animals
Puppy – G
Kitten – H
Foal – E
Calf – F
Lamb – D
Cub – A
Kid – C
Fawn – B

page 28 – Red Riding Hood
Squares H6 and C2 are the same.

page 30 – Santa's Elves
1. There are five elves in the picture
2. A teddy bear
3. Four parcels
4. A watch
5. Two reindeer
6. A sprig of holly

page 32 – Which Fairy?
Fairy B

page 38 – Princess in the Tower

page 46 – Tea Party

Two candy canes are on the table in picture D.

page 50 – Find the Girls

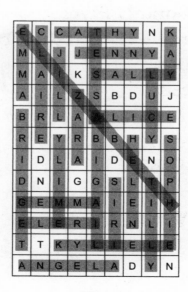

159

page 58 – Pixies Going Walkies
Poppy – Riley, Patrick – Rover, Posie – Rex, Philip – Roger

page 60 – Patchwork Quilt
There are eight different patterns.

page 62 – Twin Unicorns
Unicorns A and D are the twins.

page 66 – Good Fairy, Bad Fairy
The good fairy gets to the animals first; the bad fairy cannot reach them.

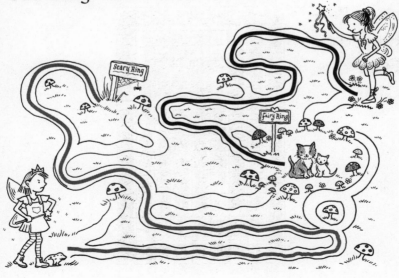

page 72 – Tiara Test
Tiara 19 is different.

page 74 – Which Is Which?
Witch A has ball 3; witch B has ball 1;
witch C has ball 2.

page 76 – How Many Words?
Here are some of the words you can
make: AIR, AIRY, AND, DAIRY, DARN,
DIARY, DIN, FAIR, FAN, FIN, FINAL,
LAIR, LAIRD, LID, RAIL.

**page 78 –
Find the
Foods**

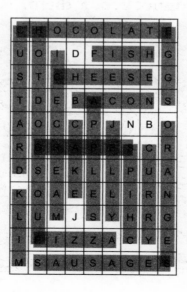

page 80 – Cinderella's Slipper

Slipper 3 is the odd one out.

page 82 – Magic Spell 1

page 86 – Odd One Out 1

Toadstool 16 is the odd one out.

page 92 – Funny Noises

A – Rrrinngg! B – Splash! C – Twang!
D – Creeeeak!

page 94 –
Find the
Boys

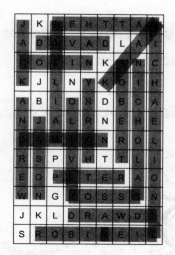

page 97 – Puss in Boots
The three squares that are the same are
K2, K5 and K6

page 98 – Riddle Me Mee
UGLY SISTERS

page 100 – Way Out

page 106 – What's Missing?

The missing things are:

1. The caterpillar
2. The spots on the toadstool
3. The butterfly
4. One of the petals on the line

page 104 Word Snake

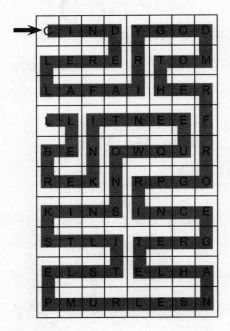

page 106 – Frog Prince

Four frogs can be turned into princes.

page 114 – Magic Spell 2

page 116 – Find the Wild Flowers

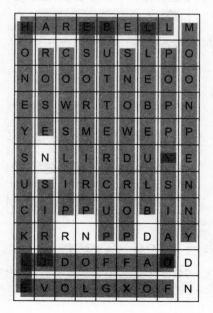

page 118 – Flower Fairies

There are 15 fairies.

page 124 – How Many Jewels?

There are 13 rubies, 18 diamonds and 27 emeralds.

page 126 – Treasure Hunt

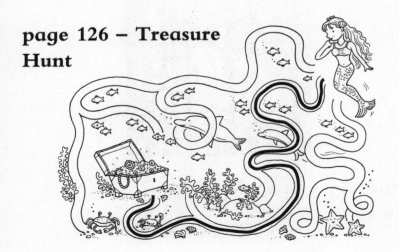

page 128 – Fairy-Tale Favourites

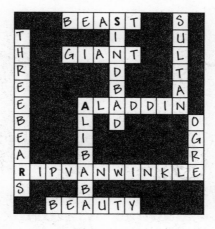

page 132 – Flying Fast

page 134 – Fairy Wands
Wands 4, 12 and 17

page 145 – Fairy Quiz

1. *Peter Pan*
2. A scratch from a spindle
3. Seven
4. Ireland
5. Her fairy godmother
6. A ring of toadstools or a ring of dark green grass on a lawn

page 144 – Bumper Wordsearch

page 148 – Odd One Out 2

Picture 7 is different because the fairy's tiara is different.

page 150 – Find the Word

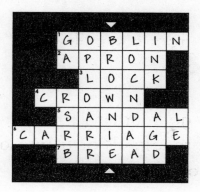

page 152 – Which Cat?

Cat 4 is different because the tag on its collar is a moon, not a star.

Nina
Fairy Ballerina

New Girl

Anna Wilson

**The first book in a magical new series about
a little fairy who brings a lot of sparkle to
everything she does – especially ballet.**

Nina Dewdrop loves ballet. And when she is accepted
into the Royal Academy of Fairy Ballet it looks like
Nina's dreams of becoming a prima fairy-ballerina are
coming true. First she has to buy everything a budding
ballerina needs, from tutus to ballet shoes. Then Nina must
say goodbye to her old fairy-friends . . .

When Nina arrives at the Academy, she instantly loves her
friendly and funny new room-mate, Peri. In the first ballet
class of term, Nina and Peri decide to perform a dance
from *Swan Lake*. But magical mayhem descends when
snooty, trouble-making Angelica Nightshade waves her
wand and tries to turn Nina into a real swan!

Princess Stories

Chosen by Anna Wilson

Every princess has a story to tell.

A pretty perfect princess and a badly behaved princess, a princess in love and a princess in BIG trouble . . .

These are just a few of the princesses on parade in this fun, magical story collection.

Gwyneth Rees
fairy dreams

Evie had always believed in fairies,
but she has never seen one . . .

When Grandma is taken into hospital, Evie finds her-
self sleeping in Grandma's old brass bed – and being
visited by Moonbeam and Star, two dream fairies
who whisk her away on a magical journey to Queen
Celeste's palace in fairyland.

Moonbeam and Star tell Evie they can't make Grandma
better, but they can give her a wonderful adventure so
long as she is sleeping in a magic bed. Can Evie find
a way to make Grandma's fairy dreams come true?

Star

Poppy Shire

The carousel music grew louder and the horses swooped through the air as they gathered speed. The breeze blew on Laura's cheeks and the fairground lights seemed to glitter and twinkle around her. To her surprise the breeze felt warm, like on a summer's day, and the air began to glow and shimmer like summery mist. She looked up and gasped. It was no longer a cool autumn evening — instead the sky was a beautiful bright blue, with the sun blazing down. And she wasn't holding on to the golden pole any more. She had real leather reins in one hand and a rope lasso in the other!

Crystal

Poppy Shire

The carousel began to spin faster, and the fairground became a blur of laughing faces. Everything started to disappear in a rainbow mist. Emily blinked. She wanted to rub her eyes, but they were going so fast, she didn't dare let go of Crystal's reins. Silvery sparkles whirled around her, and the rainbow colours of the fairground changed to dazzling white. Everything shone and glittered with light, and Emily gasped out loud. This wasn't the fairground any more. She and Crystal were in the middle of a snowstorm!

More Fairy Poems

Clare Bevan

Do you believe in fairies?

In this gorgeous collection of fairy poems you can find out all about fairy fashion, join in with the Lily-pad Prance, learn the fairy alphabet and how to do a spell to mend broken wings.

What the Autumn Fairy Wears

A cobweb coat as pale as fog,
Twiggy buttons (from a log),
Tights dyed blue with juicy berries,
Gloves as red as glossy cherries,
An oak-leaf hat in golden shades
(Spellbound so it never fades)
And spiky shoes with ivy laces,
Light and tight for treetop races.

A selected list of titles available from Macmillan Children's Books

The prices shown below are correct at the time of going to press. However, Macmillan Publishers reserves the right to show new retail prices on covers, which may differ from those previously advertised.

Nina Fairy Ballerina: New Girl Anna Wilson	ISBN: 978-0-330-43985-5	£3.99
Princess Stories Chosen by Anna Wilson	ISBN: 978-0-330-43797-4	£4.99
Fairy Dreams Gwyneth Rees	ISBN: 978-0-330-43476-8	£4.99
Magic Pony Carousel: Star Poppy Shire	ISBN: 978-0-330-44043-1	£3.99
Magic Pony Carousel: Crystal Poppy Shire	ISBN: 978-0-330-44597-9	£3.99
More Fairy Poems Clare Bevan	ISBN: 978-0-330-43935-0	£3.99

All Pan Macmillan titles can be ordered from our website, www.panmacmillan.com, or from your local bookshop and are also available by post from:
Bookpost, PO Box 29, Douglas, Isle of Man IM99 1BQ
Credit cards accepted. For details:
Telephone: 01624 677237
Fax: 01624 670923
Email: bookshop@enterprise.net
www.bookpost.co.uk

Free postage and packing in the United Kingdom